Presented to:

Bob & Myrna

From:

A Gift For You

From Canadian University College

www.cauc.ca

Project Manager: Lisa Stilwell
Designed by Mary Hooper

ISBN-13: 978-1-4041-8670-5

Printed and bound in China

www.thomasnelson.com

09 10 11 12 [HH] 6 5 4 3 2 1

Comfort

the
from WORD of PROMISE.

Reassuring Passages *from the* Psalms

THOMAS NELSON
Since 1798

NASHVILLE DALLAS MEXICO CITY RIO DE JANEIRO BEIJING

I WILL PRAISE YOU
O LORD

with my whole heart;
I will tell of all Your
marvelous works.
I will be glad and rejoice
in You; I will sing praise
to Your name,
O Most High.

(vv 1—2)

The LORD also will be a refuge
for the oppressed,
A refuge in times of trouble.
And those who know Your name
will put their trust in You;
For You, LORD, have not forsaken
those who seek You.

Sing praises to the LORD, who dwells in Zion!
Declare His deeds among the people.
When He avenges blood, He remembers them;
He does not forget the cry of the humble.

Have mercy on me, O LORD!
Consider my trouble from those
who hate me,
You who lift me up from the gates
of death,

That I may tell of all Your praise
In the gates of the daughter of Zion.

I will rejoice in Your salvation.

(vv 9—14)

PSALM 130

Out of the depths

I have cried to you, O LORD;

LORD, hear my voice!
 Let Your ears be attentive
 To the voice of my supplications.

(vv 1—2)

I wait for the LORD, my soul waits,
And in His word I do hope.

My soul waits for the LORD

More than those who watch
for the morning—
Yes, more than those who watch
for the morning.

(vv 5—6)

"*For* the oppression of the *poor,* for the sighing of the needy, Now I will arise," says the LORD; "I will set him in the safety for which he yearns."

The words of the LORD are pure words,
Like silver tried in a furnace of earth,
Purified seven times.
You shall keep them, O LORD,
You shall preserve them

from this generation

forever.

(vv 5—7)

PRESERVE ME,

O God, for in You I put my trust.

O my soul, you have said to the LORD,
    "You are my Lord,
    My goodness is nothing
      apart from You."
As for the saints who are on the earth,
  "They are the excellent ones,
    in whom is all my delight."

(vv 1—3)

I will bless the LORD who has given me counsel;
　My heart also instructs me in the night seasons.
I have set the LORD always before me;
　Because He is at my right hand I shall not be moved.

Therefore my heart is glad, and my glory rejoices;
　My flesh also will rest in hope.
For You will not leave my soul in Sheol,
　Nor will You allow Your Holy One to see corruption.
You will show me the path of life;

In Your presence is fullness of joy;
At your right hand are pleasures

forevermore.

(VV 7–11)

Blessed

IS THE MAN,

Who walks not in the
counsel of the ungodly,
Nor stands in the path of sinners,
Nor sits in the seat of the scornful;

But his delight is in the law of the LORD,
     And in His law he meditates day and night.
He shall be like a tree
     Planted by the rivers of water,
     That brings forth its fruit in its season,
     Whose leaf also shall not wither;

And whatever he does

shall prosper.

(vv 1–3)

HEAR ME *when I call,*
O God of my righteousness!

You have relieved me
in my distress;
Have mercy on me,
and hear my prayer.

(vv 1—3)

There are many who say,
"Who will show us any good?"
LORD, lift up the light of
Your countenance upon us.

You have put gladness in my heart,
More than in the season that
   their grain and wine increased.
I will both lie down in peace, and sleep;

For you alone, O LORD,

Make me dwell in safety.

(vv 6–8)

I have called UPON YOU,

for You will hear me, O God;
Incline Your ear to me,
and hear my speech.
Show Your marvelous lovingkindness
by Your right hand,
You who save those who trust in You
From those who rise up against them.
Keep me as the apple of Your eye;
Hide me under the shadow
of Your wings.

(vv 6—8)

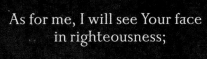

As for me, I will see Your face
in righteousness;

I shall be satisfied

when I awake in your likeness.

(v 15)

YOUR TESTIMONIES
are wonderful;

Therefore my soul keeps them.
The entrance of Your words gives light;
It gives understanding to the simple.

I opened my mouth and panted,
    For I longed for Your commandments.
Look upon me and be merciful to me,
    As Your custom is toward those
        who love Your name.
Direct my steps by Your word,
    And let no iniquity have
        dominion over me.
Redeem me from the oppression of man,
    That I may keep Your precepts.
Make Your face shine upon Your servant,
    And teach me Your statutes.

(vv 129—135)

I cry out with my whole heart;
    Hear me, O LORD!
    I will keep Your statutes.
I cry out to You;
    Save me, and I will keep Your testimonies.
I rise before the dawning of the morning,
    And cry for help;
    I hope in Your word.
My eyes are awake through the night watches,
    That I may meditate on Your word.

Hear my voice
    according to Your lovingkindness;
O LORD, revive me according
        to Your justice.

(VV 14—16)

I WILL LOVE YOU

O LORD, my strength.

*The LORD is my rock and my
     fortress and my deliverer;
My God, my strength,
     in whom I will trust;
My shield and the horn of my salvation,
     my stronghold.
I will call upon the LORD,
     who is worthy to be praised;
So shall I be saved
     from my enemies.*

(vv 1–3)

For You will light my lamp;
The LORD my God will
enlighten my darkness.
For by You I can run against a troop,
By my God I can leap over a wall.
As for God, His way is perfect;
The word of the LORD is proven;
He is a shield to all who trust in Him.

(vv 28—30)

It is God who arms me with strength,
And makes my way perfect.

He makes my feet like the feet of deer,

And sets me on my

high places.

(vv 32—33)

PSALM 20

May the LORD,

ANSWER YOU

in the day of trouble;

May the name of the God of Jacob defend you;
May He send you help from the sanctuary,
And strengthen you out of Zion;

(vv 1—2)

May He grant you according to your heart's desire,
   And fulfill all your purpose.
We will rejoice in your salvation,
   And in the name of our God we will set up our banners!
   May the LORD fulfill all your petitions.

Now I know that

the LORD, saves His anointed;

He will answer him from His holy heaven
With the saving strength of His right hand.

(vv 4—6)

PSALM 146

HAPPY *is He*

who has the God of Jacob for his help,
Whose hope is in the LORD his God.

(v 5)

The LORD opens the eyes of the blind;
   The LORD raises those who are bowed down;
   The LORD loves the righteous.
The LORD watches over the strangers;
   He relieves the fatherless and widow;

(vv 8—9)

Praise the Lord!

PRAISE THE LORD,
   OH MY SOUL!

While I live I will praise the LORD;
I will sing praises to my God
while I have my being.

(vv 1—2)

The LORD, is my shepherd;

I shall not want.

He makes me to lie down in green pastures;
　　He leads me beside the still waters.
He restores my soul;
　　He leads me in the paths of righteousness
　　For His name's sake.

(vv 1—3)

You prepare a table before me
    in the presence of my enemies;
  You anoint my head with oil;
  My cup runs over.
Surely goodness and mercy shall follow me
  All the days of my life;

And I will dwell in the house
    of the LORD,
forever.

(vv 5—6)

PSALM 138

I WILL WORSHIP
toward Your holy temple,

And praise Your name
For Your lovingkindness
   and Your truth;
For You have magnified Your word
   above all Your name.
In the day when I cried out,
         You answered me,
And made me bold with
      strength in my soul.

(vv 2—3)

Though I walk in the midst of trouble,
You will revive me;
You will stretch out Your hand
Against the wrath of my enemies,
And Your right hand will save me.
The Lord will perfect that which concerns me;

Your mercy, Oh Lord,
endures forever;
Do not forsake the works
of Your hands.

(vv 7—8)

TO YOU, *O LORD,*
I LIFT UP MY SOUL.

O my God, I trust in You.

(vv 1-2)

Show me Your ways, O LORD;
   Teach me Your paths.
Lead me in Your truth and teach me,
   For You are the God of my salvation;
   On You I wait all the day.
Remember, O LORD, Your tender mercies
   and Your lovingkindnesses,
   For they are from of old.
Do not remember the sins of my youth,
   nor my transgressions;
   According to Your mercy remember me,
   For Your goodness' sake, O LORD.

(vv 4—7)

All the paths of the LORD are mercy and truth,
To such as keep His covenant and
His testimonies.

(v 10)

The secret of the LORD is with those who fear Him,
And He will show them His covenant.
My eyes are ever toward the LORD,
For He shall pluck my feet out of the net.

(vv 14-15)

Keep my soul, and deliver me;
Let me not be ashamed,
for I put my trust in You.

Let integrity and uprightness preserve me,
FOR I WAIT *for You.*

(vv 20–21)

The LORD, *is my light*
AND MY SALVATION;

Whom shall I fear?
The LORD *is the strength of my life;*
Of whom shall I be afraid?

(v 1)

One thing I have desired of the LORD,
That will I seek:
That I may dwell in the house of the LORD
All the days of my life,
To behold the beauty of the LORD,
And to inquire in His temple.
For in the time of trouble
He shall hide me in His pavilion;
In the secret place of His tabernacle
He shall hide me;
He shall set me high upon a rock.

(vv 4—5)

Hear, O LORD, when I cry with my voice!
 Have mercy also upon me, and answer me.
When You said, "Seek My face,"
 My heart said to You, "Your face, LORD,
  I will seek."
Do not hide Your face from me;
 Do not turn Your servant away in anger;
 You have been my help;
 Do not leave me nor forsake me,
 O God of my salvation.
When my father and my mother forsake me,
 Then the Lord will take care of me.

(vv 7–10)

I would have lost heart, unless I had believed
 That I would see the goodness of the LORD
 In the land of the living.
Wait on the LORD; Be of good courage,

And He shall strengthen your heart;
Wait, I SAY, ON THE LORD!

(vv 13–14)

I will extol You, O LORD,

for You have lifted me up,
And have not let my foes
rejoice over me.

O LORD my God, I cried out to You,
And You healed me.
O LORD, You brought my soul up from the grave;
You have kept me alive, that I should not
go down to the pit.

Sing praise to the LORD, you saints of His,
    And give thanks at the remembrance
        of His holy name.
For His anger is but for a moment,
    His favor is for life;
    Weeping may endure for a night,
But joy comes in the morning.

(vv 1—5)

You have turned for me
    my mourning into dancing;
    You have put off my sackcloth and
        clothed me with gladness,
To the end that my glory may sing praise to You
    and not be silent.

O LORD my God, I will give thanks to You
forever.

(vv 11—12)

PSALM 139

O LORD,

YOU HAVE SEARCHED ME

and known me.

You know my sitting down and my rising up;
    You understand my thought afar off.
You comprehend my path and my lying down,
    And are acquainted with all my ways.
For there is not a word on my tongue,
    But behold, O LORD, You know it altogether.
You have hedged me behind and before,
    And laid Your hand upon me.
Such knowledge is too wonderful for me;
    It is high, I cannot attain it.

(vv 1—6)

Where can I go from Your Spirit?
    Or where can I flee from Your presence? . . .
If I say, "Surely the darkness shall fall on me,"
    Even the night shall be light about me;
Indeed, the darkness shall not hide from You,
    But the night shines as the day;
    The darkness and the light are both alike to You.

(vv 7, 11–12)

SEARCH ME, O GOD,
and know my heart;

Try me, and know my anxieties;
And see if there is any wicked way in me,

And lead me
in the way everlasting.

(vv 23–24)

PSALM 33

BEHOLD
the eye of the LORD,

is on those who fear Him,
On those who hope in His mercy,
To deliver their soul from death,
And to keep them alive in famine.

Our soul waits for the LORD;
  He is our help and our shield.
For our heart shall rejoice in Him,
  Because we have trusted in His holy name.
Let Your mercy, O LORD, be upon us,
  Just as we hope in You.

(vv 18—22)

Sing to Him
a new song;

Play skillfully with a shout of joy.

(v 3)

Oh, taste and see that

THE LORD IS GOOD;

Blessed is the man who trusts in Him!

Oh, fear the LORD, you His saints!
    There is no want to those who fear Him.

(vv 8—9)

The righteous cry out, and the LORD hears,

    And delivers them out of all their troubles.
    The Lord is near to those who have a
      broken heart,
    And saves such as have a contrite spirit.

(vv 17—18)

The LORD redeems the soul of His servants,
And none of those who trust in Him
shall be condemned.

(v 22)

Oh, *magnify* the LORD *with me,*

And let us *exalt His name*

together.

(v 3)

PSALM 37

TRUST IN THE LORD,
and do good;

Dwell in the land, and
    feed on His faithfulness.
Delight yourself also in the LORD,
And He shall give you the desires
    of your heart.

Commit your way to the LORD,
    Trust also in Him,
And He shall bring it to pass.
    He shall bring forth your righteousness
    as the light,

And your justice
        as the noonday.

(vv 3–6)

I WILL LIFT UP MY EYES

to the hills —

From whence comes my help?
My help comes from the LORD,
Who made heaven and earth.

He will not allow your foot to be moved;
   He who keeps you will not slumber.
Behold, He who keeps Israel
   Shall neither slumber nor sleep.

The LORD is your keeper;
   The LORD is your shade at your right hand.
The sun shall not strike you by day,
Nor the moon by night.

The LORD shall preserve you from all evil;
   He shall preserve your soul.
The LORD shall preserve your going out
   and your coming in

From this time forth, and even
forevermore.

PSALM 40

I WAITED

patiently for the LORD;

And He inclined to me,
And heard my cry.

He also brought me up
    out of a horrible pit,
Out of the miry clay,
And set my feet upon a rock,
And established my steps.

(vv 1—2)

Many, O LORD my God, are Your
wonderful works
Which You have done;
And Your thoughts toward us
Cannot be recounted to You in order;
If I would declare and speak of them,
They are more than can be numbered.

(v 5)

Let all those who seek You rejoice
and be glad in You;
Let such as love Your salvation
say continually,
"The LORD be magnified!"
But I am poor and needy;
Yet the LORD thinks upon me.

You are my help and my deliverer;

Do not delay, O my God.

(vv 16—17)

PSALM 46

God is our refuge
AND STRENGTH,
A very present help in trouble.

Therefore we will not fear,
Even though the earth be removed,
And though the mountains be carried
into the midst of the sea;
Though its waters roar and be troubled,
Though the mountains shake
with its swelling.

(vv 1—3)

There is a river whose streams shall
      make glad the city of God,
The holy place of the tabernacle
      of the Most High.
God is in the midst of her, she shall not be moved;
      God shall help her, just at the break of dawn.
The nations raged, the kingdoms were moved;
      He uttered His voice, the earth melted.
The LORD of hosts is with us;
      The God of Jacob is our refuge.

(vv 4—7)

Be still, and know that I am God;
      I will be exalted among the nations,
      I will be exalted in the earth!

The LORD *of hosts is with us;*
THE GOD OF JACOB
is our refuge.

(vv 10—11)

PSALM 51

HAVE MERCY
upon me, O God,
According to Your lovingkindness;

According to the multitude
of Your tender mercies,
Blot out my transgressions.
Wash me thoroughly from my iniquity,
And cleanse me from my sin.

(vv 1—2)

Create in me a clean heart, O God,
    And renew a steadfast spirit within me.
Do not cast me away from Your presence,
    And do not take Your Holy Spirit from me.

Restore to me the joy of Your salvation,
    And uphold me by Your generous Spirit.

(vv 10—12)

O Lord, open my lips,
    And my mouth shall show forth Your praise.
For You do not desire sacrifice, or else I would give it;
    You do not delight in burnt offering.
The sacrifices of God are a broken spirit,
    A broken and a contrite heart—

These, O God,

You will not despise.

(vv 14—17)

In You, O Lord,

I PUT MY TRUST;

Let me never be put to shame.

Deliver me in Your righteousness,
    and cause me to escape;
    Incline Your ear to me, and save me.
Be my strong refuge,
    To which I may resort continually;
    You have given the commandment
        to save me,
    For You are my rock and my fortress.

(vv 1—3)

For You are my hope, O Lord God;
    You are my trust from my youth.
By You I have been upheld from birth;
    You are He who took me out
        of my mother's womb.

My praise shall be continually of You.
I have become as a wonder to many,
But You are my strong refuge.
Let my mouth be filled with Your praise
And with Your glory all the day.

(vv 5—8)

But I will hope continually,
And will praise You yet more and more.
My mouth shall tell of Your righteousness
And Your salvation all the day,
For I do not know their limits.
I will go in the strength of the Lord God;
I will make mention of Your righteousness,
of Yours only.

O God, You have taught me from my youth;
And to this day I declare Your wondrous works.

(vv 14—17)

My lips shall greatly rejoice
when I sing to you,
And my soul, which You
have redeemed. (v 23)

PSALM 91

HE *who dwells*

in the secret place of the Most High
Shall abide under the shadow
of the Almighty.

I will say of the Lord, "He is my
    refuge and my fortress;
    My God, in Him I will trust."
Surely He shall deliver you
    from the snare of the fowler
    And from the perilous pestilence.
He shall cover you with His feathers,
    And under His wings you
      shall take refuge;
His truth shall be your shield
    and buckler.

(vv 1—4)

Because you have made the LORD,
    who is my refuge,
      Even the Most High, your dwelling place,
No evil shall befall you,
    Nor shall any plague come
      near your dwelling;

For He shall give His angels charge over you,
    To keep you in all your ways.

In their hands they shall bear you up,
    Lest you dash your foot against a stone.

(vv 9–12)

"Because he has set his love upon Me,
    therefore I will deliver him;
I will set him on high, because he
    has known My name.
He shall call upon Me, and I will answer him;
    I will be with him in trouble;
    I will deliver him and honor him.

With long life I will satisfy him,

And show Him My salvation.

(vv 14–16)

Oh, give thanks

to the LORD, for He is good!
For His mercy endures forever.

(v 1)

I called on the LORD in distress;
The LORD answered me and
set me in a broad place.
The LORD is on my side;
I will not fear.
What can man do to me?
The LORD is for me
among those who help me;
Therefore I shall see my desire
on those who hate me.
It is better to trust in the LORD
Than to put confidence in man.
It is better to trust in the LORD
Than to put confidence in princes.

(vv 5—9)

Open to me the gates of righteousness;
    I will go through them,
    And I will praise the LORD.
This is the gate of the LORD,
    Through which the righteous shall enter.
I will praise You,
    For You have answered me,
    And have become my salvation.

(vv 19–21)

Oh, give thanks to the LORD,
        for He is good!

For His mercy endures

forever.

(v 1)

PSALM 57

BE MERCIFUL TO ME,
O God, be merciful to me!

For my soul trusts in You;
And in the shadow of Your wings
I will make my refuge,
Until these calamities have passed by.

I will cry out to God Most High,
    To God who performs all things for me.
He shall send from heaven and save me;

(vv 1—3)

I will praise You, O LORD, among the peoples;
    I will sing to You among the nations.
For Your mercy reaches unto the heavens,
    And Your truth unto the clouds.

Be exalted, O God, above the heavens;
    Let Your glory be above all the earth.

Let Your glory
        be above all the earth.

(vv 9—10)

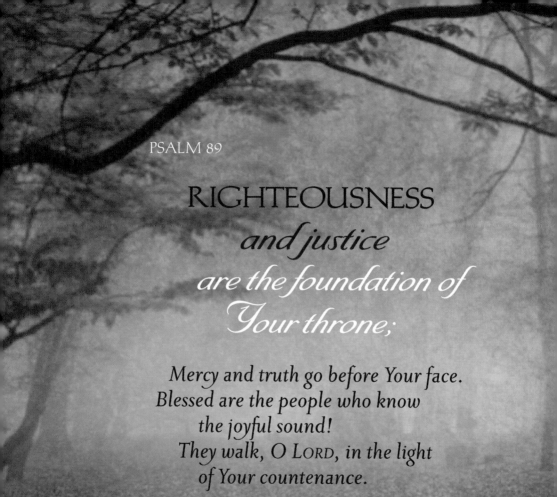

PSALM 89

RIGHTEOUSNESS
and justice
are the foundation of
Your throne;

Mercy and truth go before Your face.
Blessed are the people who know
the joyful sound!
They walk, O Lord, in the light
of Your countenance.

In Your name they rejoice all day long,
  And in Your righteousness they are exalted.
For You are the glory of their strength,
  And in Your favor our horn is exalted.

*For our shield belongs
        to the LORD,*

And our kind to the
  Holy One of Israel.

(vv 3–6)

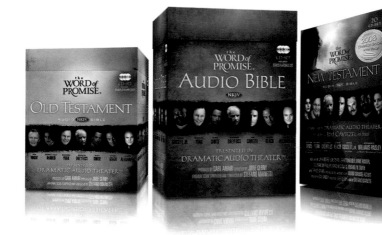

HEAR THE BIBLE COME ALIVE!

A star-studded cast of over 600 actors, original music score, and incredible sound effects combine to create a dramatic audio theater experience that makes you feel like you're really there with Abraham, Moses, & Jesus. Listen in your car, on your MP3 player, or with your family or small group to gain a new perspective of the Bible.

The Word of Promise® Audio Bible, Old Testament, & New Testament are available wherever books & Bibles are sold.

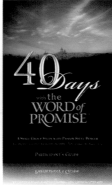

*Listen
to the entire*
New
Testament
in just
40 days!

Enjoy the dramatic audio theater of *The Word of Promise® New Testament Audio Bible* for 30 minutes a day and experience the complete New Testament in only 40 days.

Turn *The Word of Promise® New Testament Audio Bible* into a small group or church-wide experience, using *40 Days with The Word of Promise®*, a study that takes a comprehensive and multimedia approach enabling families, churches, and small groups to listen to and study the New Testament together. The small group or church-wide campaign includes video discussion starters, sermon outlines, small group guides, and other downloadable resources.

- CD Table *of* Contents -